CW00376201

C B D

{COCKTAILS}

THE LONDON BOTANISTS

C B D

{COCKTAILS}

A guide to the best
CBD cocktail recipes:

Where to find them
and how to make them

- DESIGNED BY -

ROOT7

Root7
Unit 201 Print Rooms,
Union Street,
SE1 0LH

First printed by Root7 in 2019

Copyright @ Root7
Text & book design by Lewis Plowman
CBD knowledge & advice provided by
David Burden & Chloe Lawrence-Green
See recipe credits on page 114

ISBN: 978-1-5272-5035-2

Printed and bound in England
Biddles Books Limited

Disclaimer:
All the information in this book is intended
as a guide and should not be used for any
medical purposes whatsoever. CBD is a
food supplement and not intended to treat,
diagnose, prevent or cure any disease.
Do not use whilst pregnant or during
breastfeeding. CBD should only be taken by
those of 18 years and over.

PREFACE

"Root7 have been designing products to brighten up your home for the last five years, from geometric glassware for entertaining to cocktail tools with a Titanium finish. Based in London, we are a sociable bunch who like to explore the various bars and hidden gems that the city has to offer. Over the years we have discussed wanting to write a cocktail book but it took a chance meeting with Dave from London Botanists whilst walking my dog last Christmas to kick it off. After learning about his CBD business we decided to meet up and hatch a plan. We hope you like where it took us....'

ROB INGRAM - ROOT7

CBD COCKTAILS

CONTENT

EDITOR
Lewis Plowman
Product Designer
ROOT7

CBD INFO
David Burden
Director
**THE LONDON
BOTANISTS**

THE LONDON BOTANISTS

The London Botanists have an extraordinary wealth of knowledge when it comes to CBD, which has been critical in the creation of this book and its recipes.

It is incredibly important to use CBD from reputable sources, to ensure that the product is wholly free from impurities.

"Whether it be with a restaurant or artisan chocolatier, we work with the very best, combining our expertly created CBD oil with their craftsmanship to elevate the benefits of CBD. Our products make use of just a few key ingredients, allowing the quality of the ingredients to speak for themselves, resulting in exceptional products. In this book we share with you a collection of superb cocktails created by 11 forward thinking restaurants and bars located around London that are helping to drive the CBD revolution forward."

**"UNDERPINNING EVERYTHING WE DO IS
AUTHENTICITY AND HONESTY"**

CBD (cannabidiol) is one of over 100 phytocannabinoids and over 400 chemical compounds extracted from the Cannabis Sativa L plant. Amongst these compounds are a mixture of cannabinoids, flavonoids, phytonutrients and terpenes – all with their own unique benefits. While the use of CBD is gaining in popularity, there is still some hesitation due to the fact that CBD is derived from Cannabis.

Cannabis, however, can be split into two different classifications; Hemp and Marijuana. Marijuana contains significant levels of Tetrahydrocannabinol (THC), the psychoactive compound that causes a 'high'. Hemp, however, contains negligible amounts of THC and cannot cause a high. All of the CBD products in this book are derived from EU approved strains of hemp containing less than 0.2% THC.

The cannabis compound that doesn't produce a high

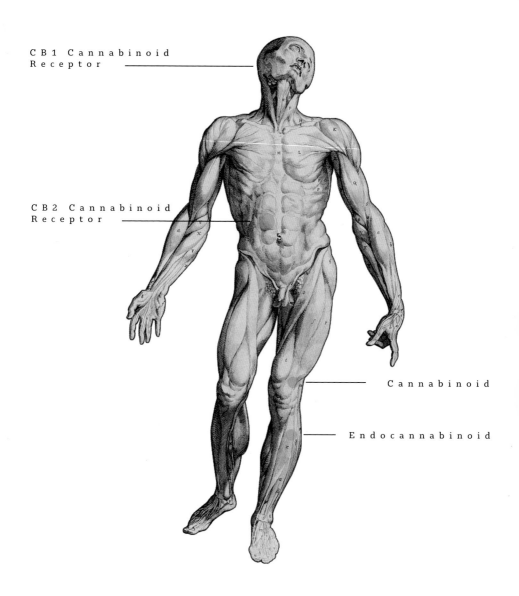

CB1 Cannabinoid
Receptor

CB2 Cannabinoid
Receptor

Cannabinoid

Endocannabinoid

INSIDE LOOK
Of Your

CB Receptors

HOW IT WORKS

THE EFFECTS OF CBD

CBD works in tandem with one of your body's systems known as the Endocannabinoid System (ECS).

The function of the ECS is to regulate stress relief, immune response and maintain homeostatic control over appetite, sleep, mood and pain. Cannabinoid receptors are capable of receiving signals from both your body's naturally produced cannabinoids and cannabinoids produced by plants, such as CBD.

Your naturally produced Endocannabinoids send signals to your ECS, which influences homeostasis. Plant based cannabinoids interact with your ECS in two ways. The first is by directly influencing your CB1 and CB2 receptors; the second is by slowing down the rate at which your enzymes break down your Endocannabinoids, giving your ECS a little boost.

KNOW YOUR
ENDOCANNABINOID SYSTEM

The ECS is made from a collection of Cannabinoid receptors located all over the body, however most are found predominantly in the brain. Your main Cannabinoid receptors are:

CB1

These are expressed most densely in the brain and central nervous system and are largely responsible for mediating the effects of cannabinoid binding in the brain.

CB2

These receptors are mainly located around your internal organs where they are primarily responsible for mediating cytokine release.

TERPENES

Terpenes are the hydrocarbon compounds found in cannabis, as well as a handful of other plants. They are the building blocks for essentials oils, which produce the smells that we commonly associate with plants, fruits and flowers.

CBD interacts with these compounds and can amplify their effects, helping the body to achieve homeostasis.

IN THE COCKTAILS

LEMON/LIME
D-LIMONENE,
NEROLIDOL

MINT
OCIMENE,
ISOPULEGOL,
PULEGONE

ROSEMARY
PINENE,
CAMPHOR,
CARYOPHYLLENE
OXIDE

APPLE
FARNESENE

ELDERFLOWER
LINALOOL

Terpenes are related to multiple beneficial effects on our bodies and well-being. They can calm you, aid with reducing inflamtion and even aid memory retention. Terpenes enhance the uplifting effects that you experience when exposed to the multi-sensory world around you. These can range from catching a whiff of the tangy rind of a lemon, to breathing in crisp air on a walk through a pine forest. Another example would be the effects of the terpene linalool from lavender essential oil. This oil relaxes you and puts you at ease whenever you smell a fresh bunch of lavender.

BENEFITS FOUND IN
COCKTAIL INGREDIENT'S TERPENES

PINENE- Bronchodilator, aids asthma, anti-inflammatory, aids memory

CAMPHOR – When applied to skin produces cooling sensation, slight local anaesthetic, anti-microbial

D-LIMONENE- Anti depressant, GRD, assists with skin absorption of other terpenes

CARYOPHYLLENE OXIDE – Anti-fungal, anti-coagulant

NEROLIDOL – Potent anti-fungal and anti-malarial properties, anti-oxidant

OCIMENE – Anti-fungal, anti-septic, decongestant, anti-bacterial

ISOPULEGOL- Gastroprotective, anti-inflammatory, reduces seizure severity in animal studies, anti-microbial

PULEGONE- Acetylcholinesterase inhibitor, aids memory

FARNESENE- Anti-inflammatory, antifungal, antibacterial, anxiety relief, antispasmodic

LINALOOL- Anti-anxiety, sedative, anti-convulsant, pain relief, anti-depressant

VEGAN
COCKTAILS

You may not have considered this, but many cocktail components have been found to be not vegan friendly, predominantly due to either their ingredients, their production processes, or both. It's also worth noting that a lot of wine and beer products are also non vegan friendly, due to how they are clarified; in a process called 'fining', which uses gelatins or fish extracts.

SUGAR

Most refined sugar is produced using bone char, which gives it a white colour. Even brown sugar (which is just white sugar with molasses added to it).

SAUCES

Honey and dairy products are obvious ingredients to avoid, but did you know that a Bloody Mary contains fish, from the Worcestershire sauce?

EGGS

Egg white is a very common cocktail ingredient, which is used to create a thick and creamy taste. We use Aquafaba as an alternative (see pg. 16).

THE MORE YOU KNOW

All of our cocktails have been designed to be vegan friendly.
If you are unable to find the suggested ingredients for vegan replacements, then it is
advised to take care when checking product labels to check if they contain any animal
products. Better yet, a quick search online will usually confirm if they are vegan friendly,
as most companies seek to be very transparent on this issue.

Woo Moo!

CBD IN TOWN

LONDON CALLING

Spread all across London, from eastern Hackney to west side Barnes, we've curated a fine selection of bars, cafe's and even a chocolatier in the name of CBD.

There is a great feeling of local community within all locations that offer CBD. Each location exudes a real warmth and authenticity from both their work and customers.

All of the brands we work with are infectiously passionate about what they do, which makes the process of working with them very exciting. Working closely with the bartenders and trialling their tasty recipes through this book has been a lot of fun. We really love what they have created and hope that you do too.

IT'S WONDERFULLY INSPIRING TO WORK WITH THEM AND SEE THEIR CREATIONS

THE
RECIPES

HICCE

THE VIBE

Hicce is a bright and airy eatery, adorned with exposed brick, that offers modern food and quirky cocktails.

LOCATION

UNIT 102,
HICCE X WOLF & BADGER,
STABLE ST,
LONDON
N1C 4DQ

Hicce is the creation of Pip Lacey and Gordy McIntyre. Friends for many years, Hicce is a dream realised for this ambitious duo. Both the space and concept has been meticulously thought out to create the ultimate dining experience. The bar manager, Anton Ruschev, is fantastically knowledgeable about all kinds of drinks and guests can expect to see a carefully curated list of biodynamic wines, craft beers and original cocktails, each chosen to bring the best out of every plate.

L . B . D .

This classic daiquiri-inspired cocktail is best enjoyed whilst relaxing pool side, with your shades, on a hot summers day.

SHARP CITRUS FLAVOUR WITH A RUM KICK

TASTE
SHARP

DIFFICULTY
2/5

GLASS
COUPETTE

Try adding grapefruit juice for an extra citrus taste

INGREDIENTS

White Rum	50ml
Lime Juice	25ml
Sugar Syrup	25ml
CBD Syrup	1 pump
Dehydrated Lime	1
Cubed Ice	1 cup

DIRECTIONS

Squeeze out the lime juice.

Give all ingredients a hard shake with cubed ice.

DOUBLE STRAIN INTO A GLASS AND ADD A SLICE OF DEHYDRATED LIME TO GARNISH.

Best made with ~ Pampero Blanco

HICCE

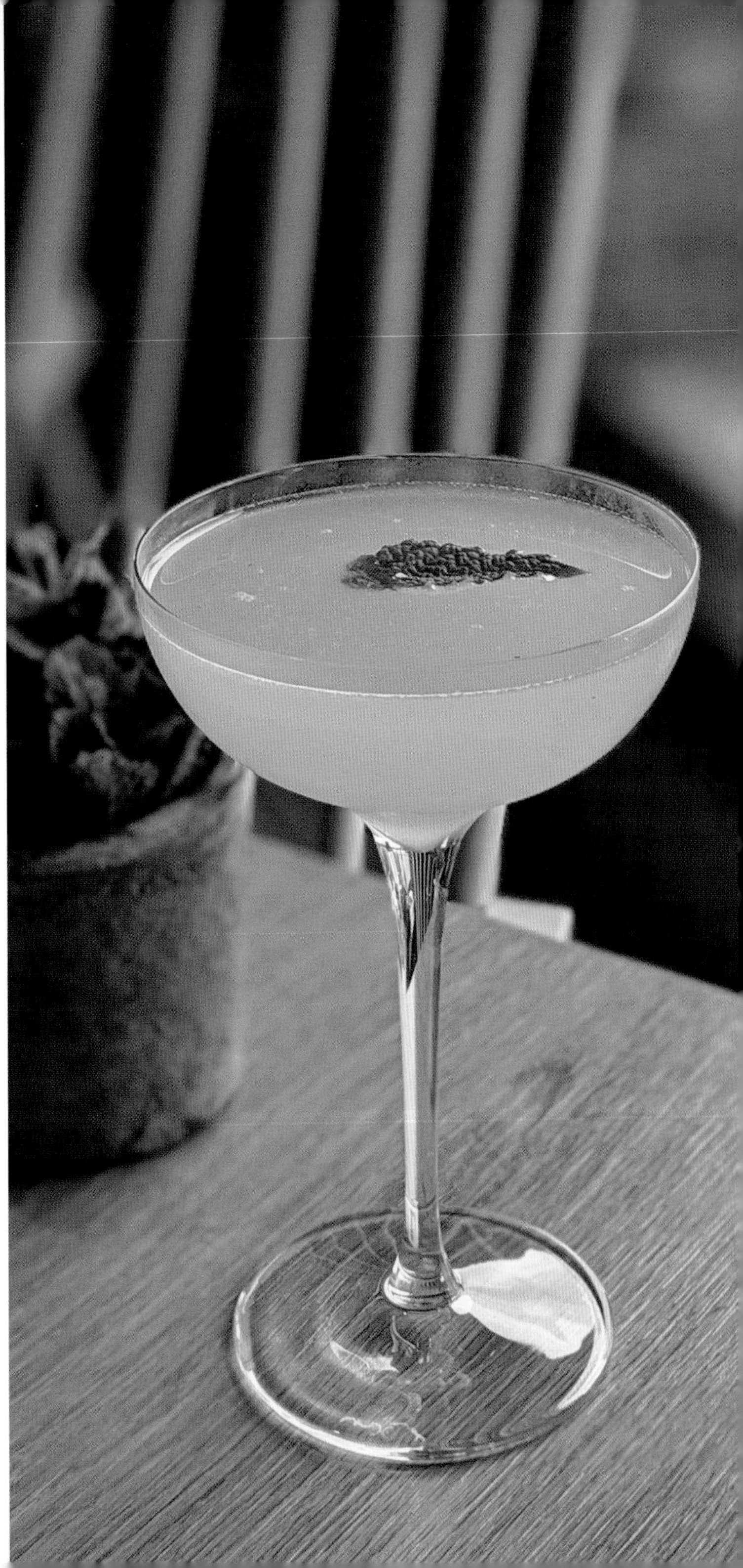

I N G R E D I E N T S

Gin	50 ml
Lemon Juice	25 ml
Sugar Syrup	25 ml
CBD Syrup	1 pump
Cubed Ice	1 cup

TASTE
SWEET

DIFFICULTY
2/5

GLASS
COUPETTE

A CLASSIC GIN-BASED COCKTAIL. CBD ENHANCES THE BOTANICAL ELEMENT TO THE DRINK.

G A R N I S H

Mint leaves	1

Best made with ~ Tanqueray Gin

D I R E C T I O N S

Add all ingredients into a cocktail
shaker and shake hard.
Double strain mixture into glass.
Slap mint in palms and add to your drink.

H O W   T O   M A K E   A   S U G A R   S Y R U P

In a medium saucepan combine equal parts sugar and water.
Bring to the boil, stirring, until the sugar has fully dissolved.
Leave this to cool and decant into an empty bottle.
Store in the fridge for up to 1 month.

T his is a mojito-based method, with the mint leaves replaced with Shiso, which adds a light touch of warming spice to the drink.

A JAPANESE TWIST

A grassy, minty & refreshing taste from the land of the rising sun

INGREDIENTS

White rum	40ml
Creme de peach	20ml
Shiso leaves	3
CBD Syrup	1 pump
Lime Juice	20ml
Vegan Honea*	10ml
Crushed Ice	1 scoop

DIRECTIONS

A dd all ingredients to a highball glass, leaving one shiso leaf for garnishing. Add a scoop of crushed ice and churn with a mixing spoon. Top with more crushed ice and garnish with a shiso leaf.

Best made with ~ Pampero Blanco

SO, WHAT IS SHISO?

Popular in Japanese cuisine the shiso leaf is from the mint family. It is sometimes known as "Beefsteak Plant" in the West, due to its purple-leaved variants. Shiso has a unique flavour, it is quite pungent, grassy and contains strong flavours of spearmint, basil, anise and cinnamon.

Honea is a bee-less, vegan honey substitute. See page 52 for more.

Kanpai

A HINT OF
JAPAN

TASTE
GRASSY

DIFFICULTY
3/5

GLASS
HIGHBALL

HICCE

27

Created as a drink to be enjoyed after dinner, made from rich botanical digestifs that nicely complement CBD.

A VEGAN FRIENDLY AMARO SOUR

TASTE	DIFFICULTY	GLASS
SWEET	3/5	COUPETTE

*Aquafaba is just a fancy word for chickpea can juice

INGREDIENTS

Amaro	50ml
Lemon Juice	25ml
Elderflower Cordial	25ml
Aquafaba*	25ml
CBD Syrup	1 pump
Angostura bitters	1 dash
Chocolate bitters	1 dash

GARNISH

Edible flower	1

DIRECTIONS

Squeeze out the lemon juice.

Dry shake all ingredients together, without the ice. Add the ice cubes to shaker and shake hard.

STRAIN INTO ICE-FILLED GLASS & ADD YOUR GARNISH.

Best made with ~ Amaro Montenegro

CHRONIC TONIC

INGREDIENTS

Tonic	125 ml
Cherry bitters	1 dash
CBD Syrup	1 pump
Cubed Ice	1 cup

TASTE
DRY

DIFFICULTY
1/5

GLASS
HIGHBALL

**A SIMPLE AND CLEAN DRINK:
LOVELY DRUNK ON IT'S OWN,
OR A GREAT BASE FOR WHITE SPIRITS.**

GARNISH

Rosemary	1 sprig

Best made with ~ Franklin & Sons Ltd. Rosemary Tonic

DIRECTIONS

Add all ingredients to glass,
and top with cubed ice.
Gently stir and garnish.

FOR A HARD VERSION

We would recommend using a premium white spirit of choice,
such as 100% Blue Agave tequila, London dry gin or a Grey Goose vodka.

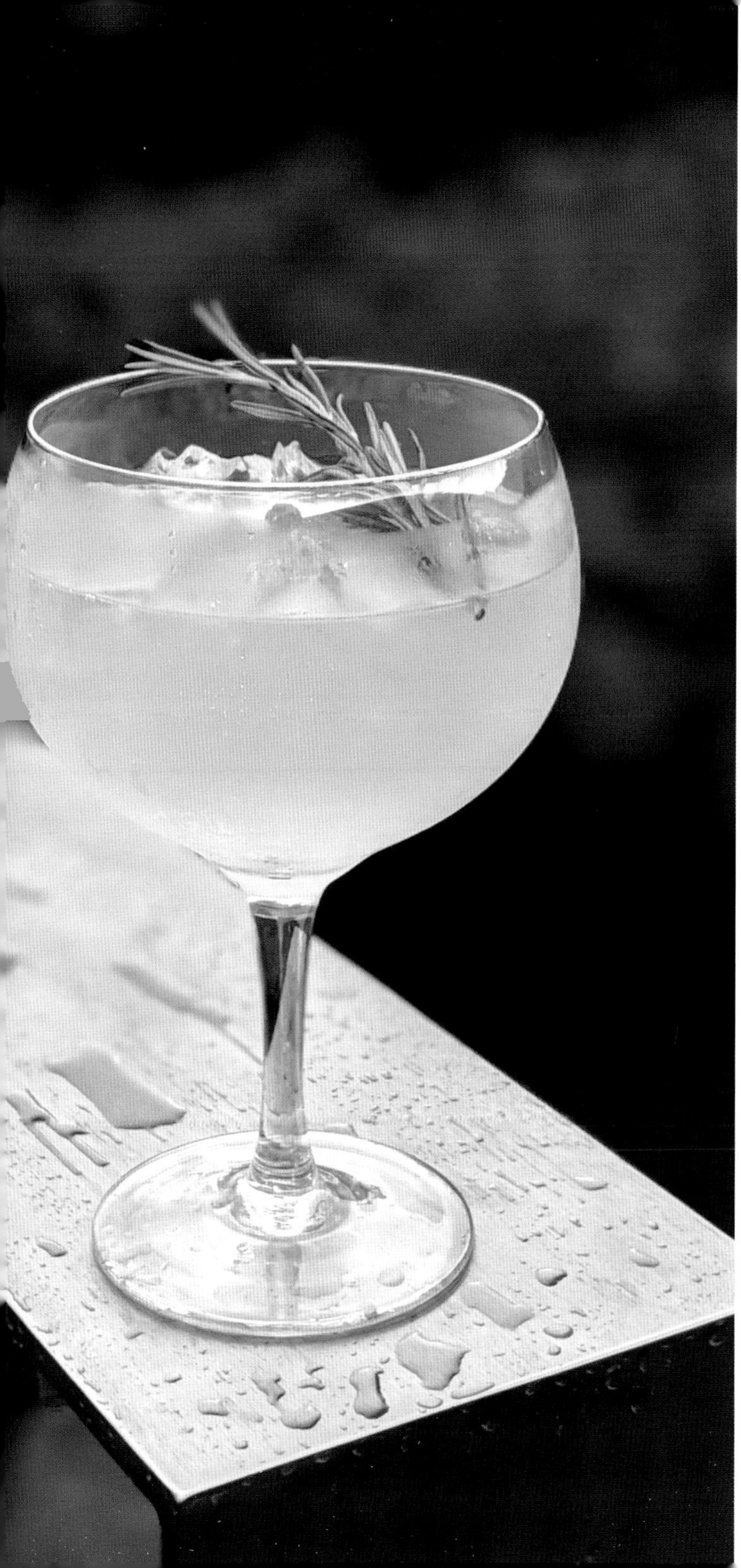

HICCE

THE BREAKFAST CLUB

THE VIBE

Retro whiskey lodge meets American speakeasy. The dimly lit basement has vintage furniture, great drinks and friendly service.

LOCATION

THE MAYOR OF SCAREDY CAT TOWN,
12-16 ARTILLERY LANE
E1 7LS
~Inside The Breakfast Club

The breakfast club in Spitalfields is tucked away on a side street opposite Liverpool Street Station. Hidden inside behind a Smeg fridge you'll find stairs leading to a secret basement bar. A great place to escape the hustle and bustle above ground.

TELL THE HOST:
"I'M HERE TO SEE THE MAYOR"

A new take on the classic margarita, with a CBD twist. Made to complement the taste of tequila, with notes of sharp lime and sweet agave.

A REFRESHING COCKTAIL WITH A KICK

TASTE
SHARP

DIFFICULTY
2/5

GLASS
TUMBLER

The cocktail's name is taken from Robert Rodriguez' third From Dusk Till Dawn movie.

INGREDIENTS

Tequila	40ml
Benedictine	10ml
Agave Syrup	15ml
Fresh Lime	10ml
CBD Syrup	1 pump

GARNISH

thyme	1 sprig
1 Dehydrated lime	

DIRECTIONS

Squeeze out the lime juice.

Add a few cubes of ice to a glass. Pour in the ingredients and stir down to chill.

TO GARNISH, ADD A SPRIG OF THYME & A WHEEL OF DEHYDRATED LIME.

Best made with ~ Chai Masala infused Don Julio blanco tequila

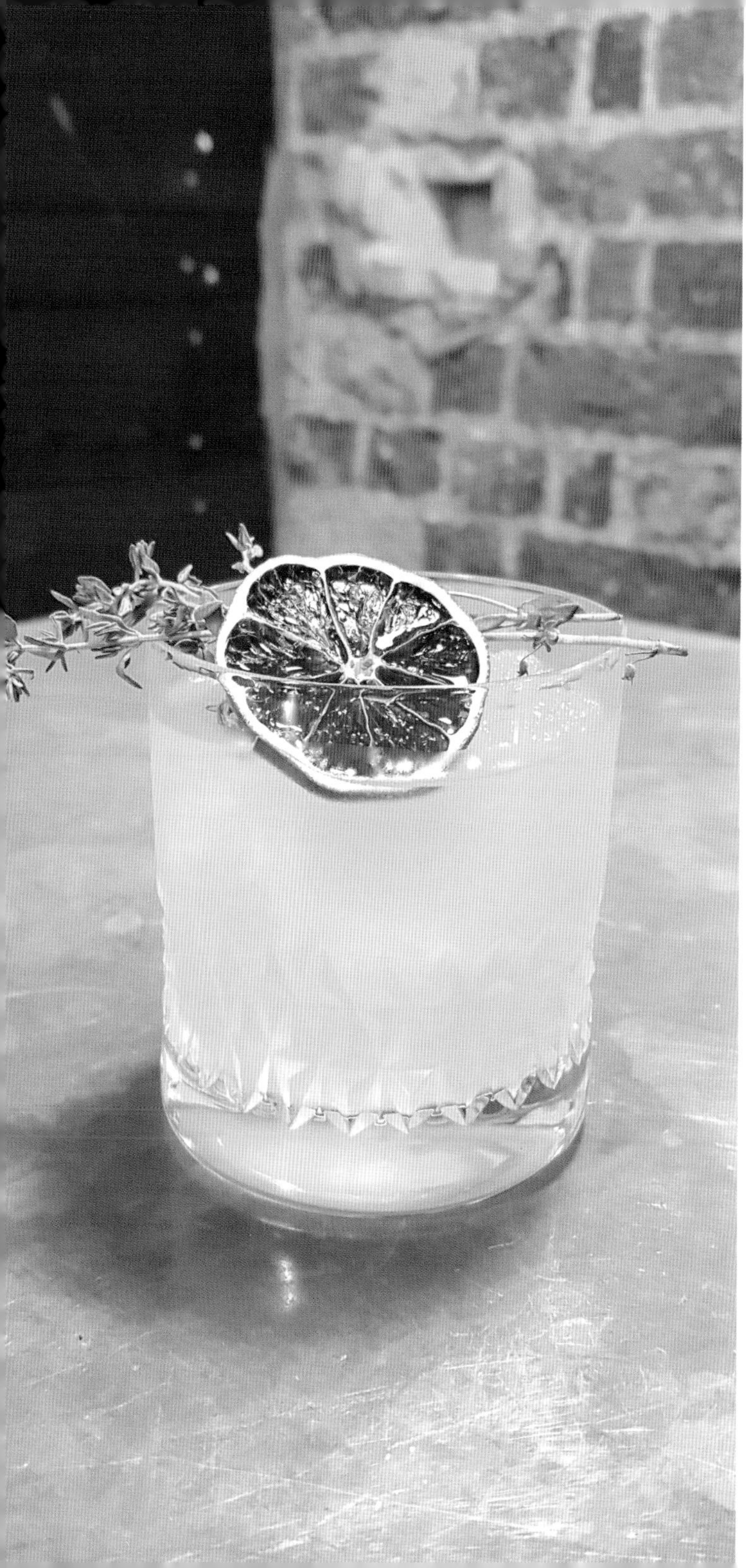

THE BREAKFAST CLUB

THE BREAKFAST CLUB

THE HIGH BOTANIST

INGREDIENTS

Gin	30ml
Violette Liqueur	10ml
Yellow Chartreuse	10ml
Green Chartreuse	10ml
CBD Syrup	1 pump

OPTIONAL

Absinthe Rinse	10ml
Edible Flower	1

TASTE
FLORAL

DIFFICULTY
3/5

GLASS
NICK & NORA

A MIX OF BOTANICAL SPIRITS ALONG WITH CBD TO CREATE A LIGHT, COMPLEX DRINK

Best made with ~ Chamomile-infused Tanqueray gin

DIRECTIONS

Stir ingredients in a mixing jar.
Pour into Nick & Nora glass,
or alternatively a wine glass.

GARNISH WITH EDIBLE FLOWER

ABSINTHE RINSE

A method for coating the inside of a glass with absinthe to add subtle aroma and taste. Add ice and 10ml of absinthe to a Nick & Nora glass, swirl it around and leave whilst preparing the cocktail. Before pouring the cocktail into the glass, give the absinthe a final swirl and then pour the ice and absinthe down the sink.

COFFEE

WAKE UP AND SMILE!

CAFFEİNE & CANNABİNOİDS

It is becoming more and more common to request the addition of a few drops of CBD in your local coffee shop and it is also becoming more common to find CBD pre-mixed into cold brew drinks. The mix of caffeine and CBD will leave you feeling alert, yet calm and can help remove the caffeine jitters brought on from too much coffee.

ESPRESSO

If you have a machine, this gives you a thicker, more bitter taste of caffeinated goodness.

COLD BREW

This is made without heat. It makes a smoother, sweeter and less acidic beverage.

DRIP / INSTANT

A great option for when you are in a rush and don't have time to brew.

CHOOSE YOUR BREW

INGREDIENTS

Vermouth	20ml
Blanco Tequila	15ml
Coffee	30ml
Tonic	50ml
CBD Syrup	1 pump

TASTE
COFFEE

DIFFICULTY
3/5

GLASS
NICK & NORA

Best made with ~
Belsazor Rose Vermouth &
Ocho Blanco Tequila

Coffee & CBD is a match made in heaven, so it only made sense to make a caffeine cocktail.

DIRECTIONS

STEP I   Shake all ingredients apart from the tonic.

STEP II   Double strain into glass and top with the tonic.

NO NEED TO GARNISH

Enjoy!

This cocktail takes inspiration from Taylor Swift, hence the name. It is calming, sweet and very tasty when incorporated with CBD.

NON - ALCOHOLIC

Try with gin if you want a hard version

INGREDIENTS

Elderflower Cordial	20ml
Apple Juice	10ml
Lemon	15ml
Elderflower Tonic	250ml
CBD Syrup	1 pump
Mint Sprig	1
Cubed Ice	1 cup

DIRECTIONS

Juice the lemon and shake together all ingredients apart from the tonic. Fill a high ball glass with cubed ice. Pour the ingredients over the ice. Top with the tonic and garnish with a mint sprig. To make an extra gorgeous drink, garnish with dehydrated lemon and an edible flower.

CHAMOMILE CORDIAL

For an extra special twist, swap the elderflower cordial for your own home made chamomile cordial. It's super easy and delicious even on it's own.

Boiled water	450ml
Honey	60ml
Fresh chamomile	2 tbsp
(Just the flower heads)	

Add chamomile flowers to a muslin steeping bag or a fine mesh tea strainer. Steep in boiled water until liquid is stained yellow and perfumed, about 20 minutes. Add the honey and stir until dissolved.

Serve it up on a hot summer day, straight from the fridge

Fresh

CHILL
OUT TIME

TASTE
SWEET

DIFFICULTY
2 / 5

GLASS
HIGHBALL

LOCATION THREE

THE
SPREAD
EAGLE

THE VIBE

A vegan, warm, comfortable and ultra-friendly pub with a gorgeous outdoor space.

LOCATION

224 HOMERTON HIGH ST,
HOMERTON,
LONDON
E9 6AS

London's first 100% vegan pub, The Spread Eagle is a friendly and relaxed hotspot that appeals to a diverse crowd of locals, regulars and patrons alike. They travel from far to visit this unique destination for its fabulous food and drink offerings.

PURPLE HAZE

This is a strong and smoky cocktail, with crisp floral notes from the lavender syrup and a refreshing dash of tangy lemon juice.

" EXCUSE ME WHILE I KISS THE SKY "

TASTE	DIFFICULTY	GLASS
FLORAL	2/5	COUPETTE

We were listening to a lot of Jimmy Hendrix that day...

INGREDIENTS

Mescal	50ml
Lemon Juice	25ml
Lavender Syrup	25ml
CBD Syrup	1 pump
Ice Cubes	2-3

GARNISH

| Edible Flower | 1 |
| Lemon Slice | 1 |

DIRECTIONS

Squeeze out the lemon juice.

Add a few cubes of ice to glass.
Shake ingredients together and serve into glass.

GARNISH WITH LEMON SLICE & EDIBLE FLOWER OR OPTIONALLY A SPRIG OF LAVENDER.

Best made with ~ Quiquiriqui Mescal

THE SPREAD EAGLE

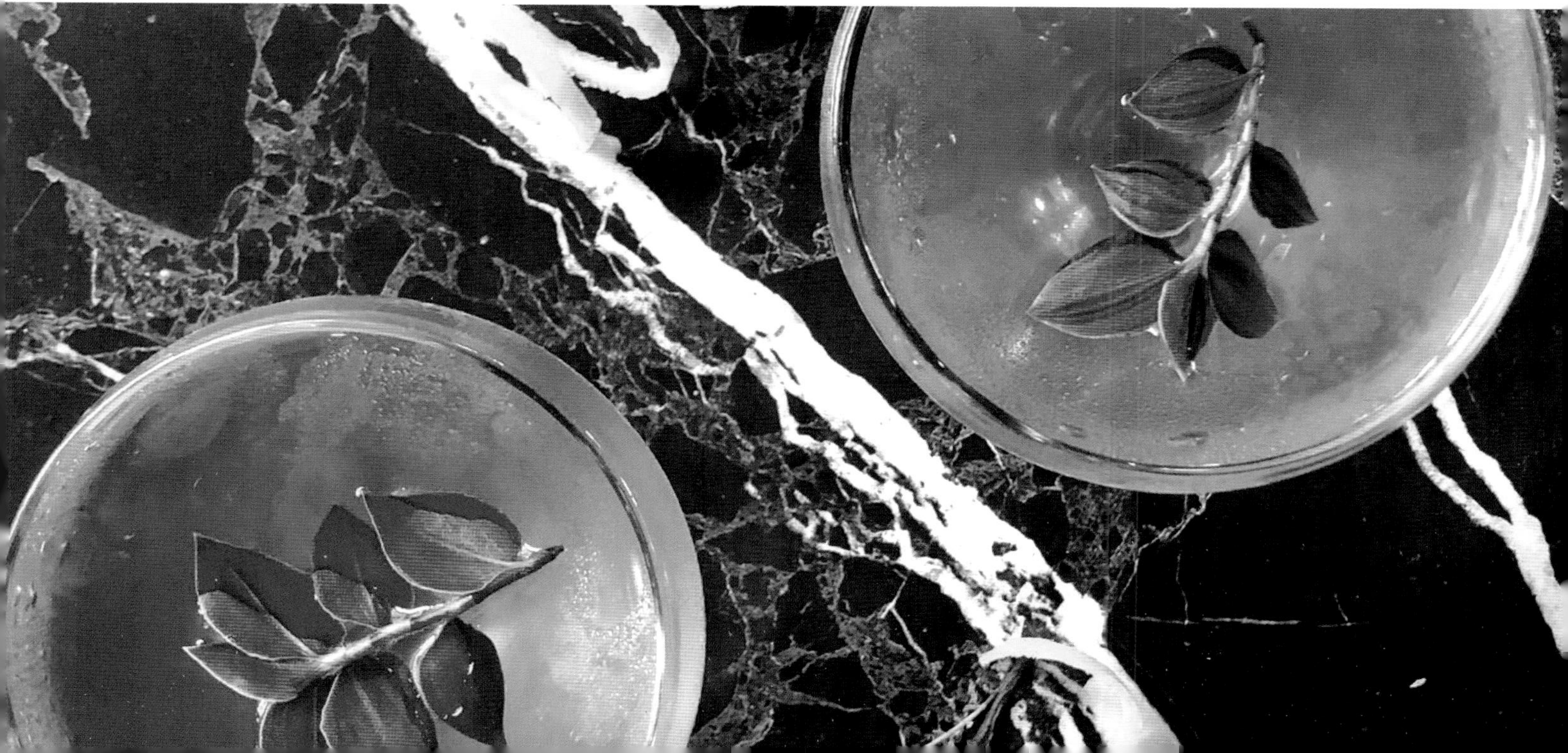

INGREDIENTS

Gin	50ml
Elderflower Cordial	25ml
Lime Juice	15ml
CBD Syrup	1 pump
Soda	100ml

TASTE
LIGHT

DIFFICULTY
2/5

GLASS
TUMBLER

OPTIONAL

Granulated Sugar	2 tsp
Matcha Powder	1 tsp

**WE DEVELOPED THIS WITH
A CLASSIC GIMLET IN MIND**

This drink is light, refreshing and elegant, with the addition of CBD and matcha sugar to give it a modern twist.

Best made with ~ The Botanist Gin

DIRECTIONS

Add a sugar rim to glass.
Squeeze out the lime juice.
Add a few cubes of ice to glass.
Shake ingredients together and serve into glass.

HOW TO MAKE A MATCHA SUGAR RIM

On a small plate, mix 1 teaspoon of matcha with 2 teaspoons of granulated sugar.
Wet the edge of your glass by running a lime wedge around it.
Gently turn the wet edge of the glass in the sugar mixture to coat the rim.

Sweet

Our signature tequila sour cocktail was developed to complement the Club Mexicana (vegan Mexican street food), that is served at the pub and uses aquafaba to replace the traditional egg white.

TRY WITH WHISKEY

Our recipe uses tequila, but it can be equally as nice with a good whiskey or bourbon.

INGREDIENTS

Tequila White	50ml
Lemon	25ml
Aquafaba	25ml
Brown Sugar	1 tsp
CBD Syrup	1 pump
Cherries	2
Slice of Lemon	1

DIRECTIONS

Cut the lemon in half. Juice one half of the lemon and add to a rocks glass with one teaspoon of brown sugar. Add the remaining ingredients to a shaker and shake well. Pour into glass, add ice cubes and mix. Garnish with cherries and a slice of lemon.

AQUAFABA

A vegan alternative to using egg whites in your whiskey sours.

You can use leftover aquafaba to make vegan cream.

Chick Peas	1 can

Drain your chick peas, keeping the juices. Whisk for 3-6 minutes using an electric whisk. The aquafaba is ready when stiff peaks start to form. This can then be made into meringue and other treats.

Tasty

VEGAN
FRIENDLY

TASTE
SOUR

DIFFICULTY
3/5

GLASS
TUMBLER

For those that don't drink, this alcohol-free recipe has an ice tea flavour and contains Kombucha and CBD. Both of these have their own significant health benefits. Kombucha is very low in sugar and rich in beneficial acids, enzymes and even antioxidants. The taste is reminiscent of green apples and citrusy fruits.

A FRESH MOCKTAIL WITH A SOUR TWIST

TASTE
SOUR

DIFFICULTY
2/5

GLASS
HIGHBALL

If you want a hard version of this cocktail, add 25ml of gin.

INGREDIENTS

Earl Grey Syrup	50ml
Lemon Juice	50ml
Original Jarr Kombucha	1 bottle
CBD Syrup	1 pump

DIRECTIONS

Squeeze out the lemon juice.

Shake ingredients together, and serve into a tall glass.

GARNISH

Mint	1 sprig
Lemon	1 slice

CLAP THE MINT IN YOUR HANDS TO RELEASE ITS FLAVOUR. ADD TO A GLASS WITH A SLICE OF FRESH LEMON.

Best made with ~ Jarr Kombucha

Jarr Man

INGREDIENTS

Gold Tequila	50ml
Triple Sec	15ml
Cider Vinegar	1 tsp
Honea	1 tsp
Warm Water	30ml
CBD Syrup	1 pump

GARNISH

Dried Orange	1 wheel

TASTE
SWEET

DIFFICULTY
2 / 5

GLASS
COUPETTE

USING CIDER VINEGAR AS THE SOUR ELEMENT, VEGAN HONEA AS THE SWEET AND CBD SYRUP TO PRODUCE AN ON-TREND FEEL TO A CLASSIC MARGARITA.

Best made with ~ El Jimador Reposado Tequila

DIRECTIONS

Mix the honea and water together until diluted.
Add ingredients to a shaker.
Shake gently and pour into a chilled glass.
Garnish with a dried orange wheel.

HONEA A BEE FRIENDLY CHOICE

Honea is a Bee-less vegan honey alternative that offers a fresh yet decadent flavour, reminiscent of the southern Mediterranean. It has an aromatic savoury profile with a natural, honey-like flavour. It's made from a mix of sugar, inulin, apple juice, natural flowers, lemon juice, orange blossom water and molasses.

Sweet

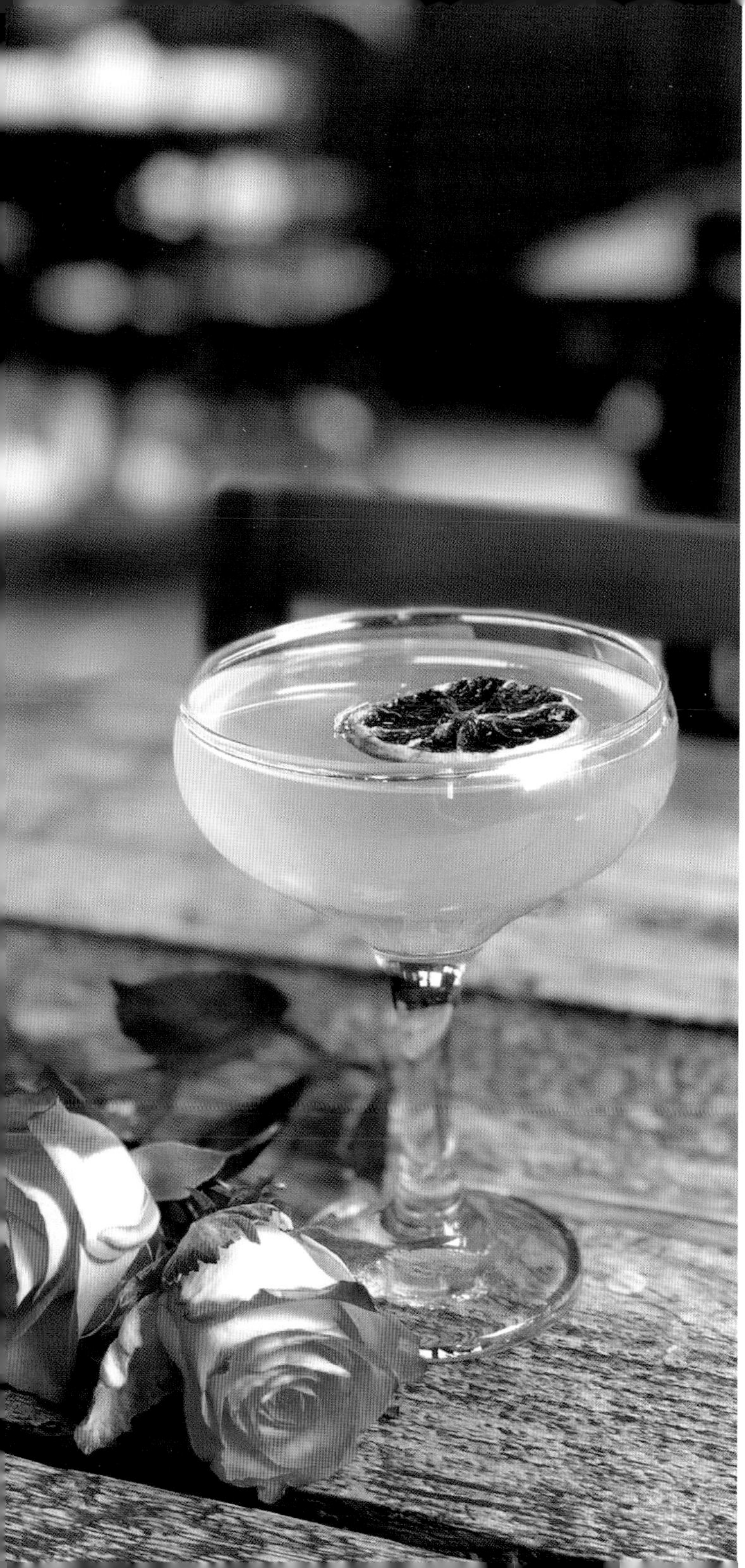

THE SPREAD EAGLE

&FEAST

THE VIBE

A cosy local cafe with tasty food, wine and of course, cocktails.

LOCATION

57 CHURCH RD,
BARNES,
LONDON
SW13 9HH

&Feast began as a small catering company in Barnes village, in 2014. It has come a long way since then, but the same values have remained at the heart of what they do: quality, taste, simplicity and passion.

BARNES MEADOW

Inspired by the abundance of rich flavours, colours, smells, as well as all the natural varieties of herbs and flowers local to Barnes Common.

COOLING WITH A SWEET AND SUBTLE FLAVOUR

TASTE	DIFFICULTY	GLASS
FLORAL	2/5	HIGHBALL

Try with meadow herbs and flowers.

INGREDIENTS

DIRECTIONS

White Rum	50ml	
Lime Juice	20ml	
Apple Juice	75ml	
Elderflower Cordial	25ml	
Mint	1 sprig	
Cucumber	4 slices	
CBD Syrup	1 pump	
Pea Syrup	1 tbsp	

Squeeze out the lime juice

Add a few cubes of ice to glass. Shake all ingredients together and serve into a highball glass.

GARNISH WITH SLICES OF CUCUMBER.

ADDING PEA SYRUP MAKES THE DRINK TURN A RICH PURPLE & PINK.

Best made with ~ White Wolf Rum

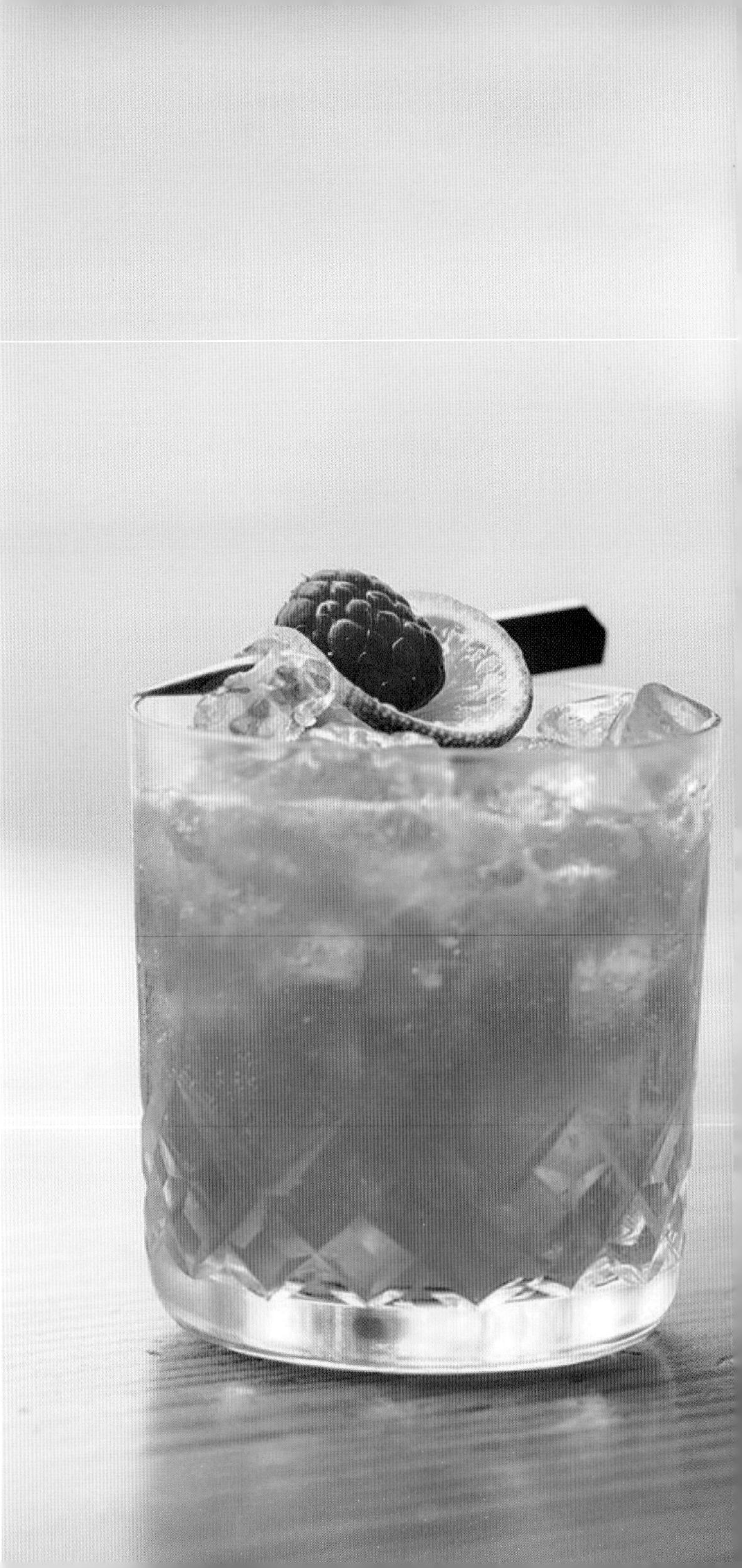

INGREDIENTS

Raspberry Syrup	40 ml
Raspberries	1 handful
Sugar	3 tsp
Lime	1 wedge
Crushed Ice	1 glass
CBD Syrup	1 pump

CHOOSE ONE

Gin	25ml
Tequila	25ml
Vodka	25ml

TASTE
SWEET

DIFFICULTY
2/5

GLASS
TUMBLER

A FRESH TAKE ON THE BRAZILIAN CLASSIC DRINK, WITH A REFRESHINGLY FRUITY TWIST.

"The Caipirinha has always been a popular choice with our catering clients, but we wanted to offer another option, with a vibrant look and taste to match."

Best made with ~ Monin Syrup

DIRECTIONS

Shake crushed ice with all ingredients including your alcohol of choice. Pour into glass and garnish with additional raspberries.

Sweet

We absolutely love using rosemary in our cooking, so wanted to infuse it into this savoury style cocktail. The flavours complement each other very well, making it the perfect aperitif cocktail.

BITTER IS BETTER

A Negroni tastes like cherry, wine and citrus, but with noticeably bitter notes.

INGREDIENTS

Campari	50 ml
Punt E Mes	25 ml
Gin	25 ml
Rosemary	1 tsp
CBD Syrup	1 pump
Orange Peel	1

DIRECTIONS

Leave ingredients over night in the fridge to infuse. Next, pour over hard ice and garnish with a spring of rosemary and orange peel. You can char the end of the rosemary to add a lovely smoky aroma to your cocktail.

Best made with ~ Sage & Apple One Gin

THE RISE OF CAMPARI

Novara, Italy - Gaspare Campari's experiments culminate with the invention of a new beverage, with a noticably distinctive bitter flavour and a secret recipe, which has remained the same until today. Campari is a symbol of intrigue and pleasure when it comes to aperitifs. The intense aroma and inspiring flavour creates a captivating and unique drinking experience.

Saluti

TASTE
DRY

DIFFICULTY
3 / 5

GLASS
TUMBLER

& FEAST

BEHIND THIS WALL

THE VIBE

An up-beat basement bar with contemporary lighting and a modern, white tiled bar.

LOCATION

411 MARE ST,
LONDON
E8 1HY

Behind This Wall is located on the top of the Narrow Way, Hackney Central. The bar was built and is run by friends with a singular approach to design, music and drinking. It has a speakeasy spirit, with the bar itself hidden away down some stairs and a large velvet curtain.

ALL INGREDIENTS ARE CAREFULLY SELECTED TO EXCLUDE ARTIFICIAL ADDITIVES, COLOURS AND FLAVOURS.

A deliciously spicy and rich version of a rum Old Fashioned. The cinnamon and pear create a lovely warming taste, perfect for relaxing beside a fire place on a cold winters night.

STRONG, RICH & COMPLEX FLAVOUR

TASTE	DIFFICULTY	GLASS
STRONG	2/5	TUMBLER

INGREDIENTS

Light Rum	35ml
Spiced Rum	20ml
Pear Calvados	1 tsp
Cinnamon Bitters	1 dash
CBD Syrup	1 pump

GARNISH

Banana Slice	1
(Fresh or crisp)	

DIRECTIONS

Add the bitters, the rum and a large single ice cube to a Tumbler.

Add a pump of CBD syrup and stir down until combined.

FLOAT THE CALVADOS ON TOP AND GARNISH WITH A BANANA SLICE.

Best made with ~
Drum & Black Spiced Rum
El Dorado 3 Year

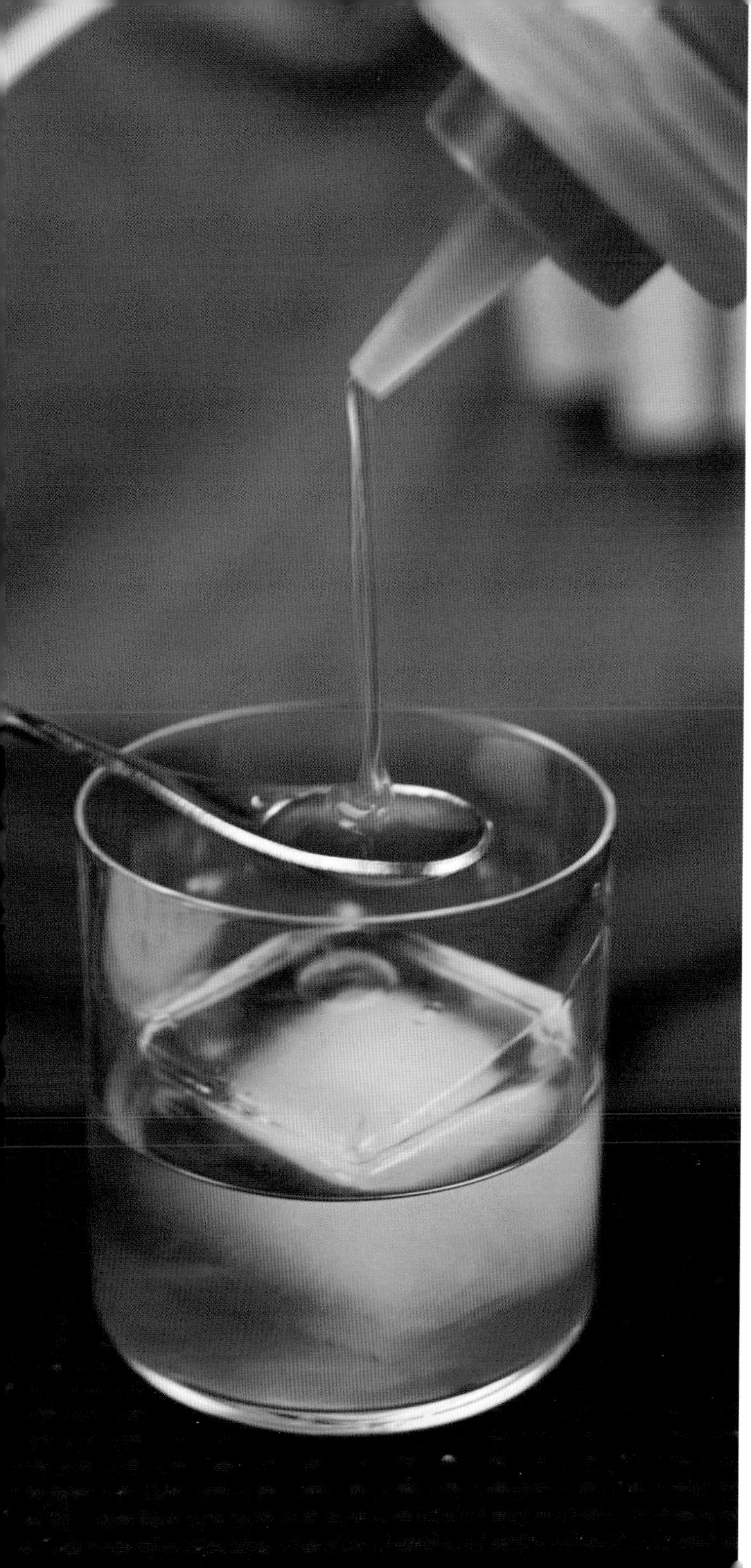

Based on a vodka daisy, with the traditional soda water swapped out for Ponzu Kombucha to complement the earthy CBD and tangy melon bitters. The resulting taste is sweet with just a touch of savoury bitterness.

KOMBUCHA COMIN' AT YA

Best made with ~ Reyka Vodka

INGREDIENTS

Vodka	45ml
Birds Botanical Spirit	15ml
Ponzu Kombucha	30ml
Melon Bitters	6 dashes
CBD Syrup	1 pump
Juniper Berries	3-5
Crushed Ice	1 glass

DIRECTIONS

Fill 2/3 of a highball glass with crushed ice. Place all the ingredients in a cocktail shaker, aside from the bitters and berries and add ice. Shake until sufficiently chilled. Double strain the ingredients into the glass, top with more crushed ice and drip the bitters over the ice to create a discernible layer. Garnish by nesting the berries in the ice.

KOMBUCHA ALTERNATIVE

If you can't make a ponzu kombucha, you could replace with a mix of equal part lime juice and pickle juice.

Brain freeze

TASTE
SWEET

DIFFICULTY
3/5

GLASS
TUMBLER

BEHIND THIS WALL

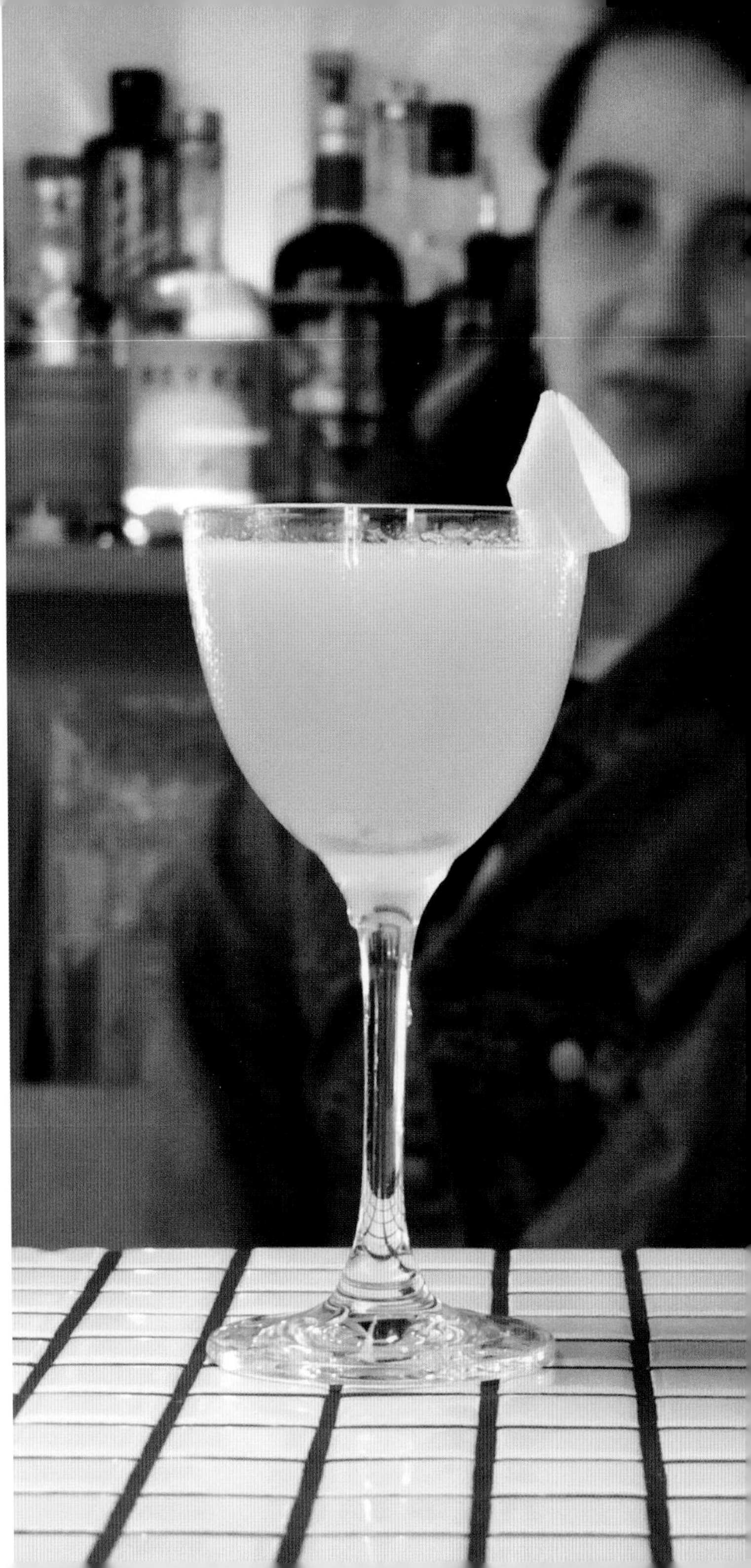

CHLOE MARTINI

A herbaceous and cleansing flavour take on the Martini.
This version of course, is shaken and not stirred.

TRY WITH JAM INFUSED GIN

TASTE
HERBY

DIFFICULTY
3/5

GLASS
NICK & NORA

To infuse gin with jam, use one bottle of gin per 110g of jam.
Combine the two in a sealed jar and leave over-night. Strain the
liquid through some muslin cloth the next day and re-bottle.

INGREDIENTS

London Dry Gin	60ml
Green Chartreuse	15ml
Lime Juice	20ml
Agave Bitters	3 dashes
CBD Syrup	1 pump

GARNISH

Lemon Zest	1 tsp

DIRECTIONS

Chill down the glass and set aside.

In a cocktail shaker, add all of the
liquid ingredients, including the
bitters, pack with ice and shake
vigorously until sufficiently chilled.

DOUBLE STRAIN THE
CONTENTS INTO YOUR
PRE-CHILLED GLASS,
GARNISH WITH LEMON
ZEST AND SERVE!

Best made with ~ Victory Gin

DREAM BAGS JAGUAR SHOES

THE VIBE

A hub for creative output that draws out like-minded people from all over the world.

LOCATION

DREAMBAGS JAGUARSHOES
32-36 KINGSLAND RD,
LONDON
E2 8DA

The unusual name is derived from the two 1980s bag and shoe wholesaler signs that hang on the buildings original store front. JAGUARSHOES COLLECTIVE constitutes of a group of creatively motivated businesses and individuals working in art, film, fashion, music, publishing and design. Their aim is to motivate positive change through creative output.

**MAKING SOMETHING,
MAKES YOU HAPPY...**

This is a cucumber and CBD version of a white Negroni which was first made in France by British bartender Wayne Collins, whilst in a pinch.

He didn't have any Campari and Vermouth, so instead reached out for Suze and Lillet (French apéritifs) and voila the white Negroni was born.

WHITE NEGRONI WITH BOTANICAL "AROMATES"

TASTE
DRY

DIFFICULTY
2/5

GLASS
TUMBLER

INGREDIENTS

Gin	25ml
Suze	25ml
Lillet Blanc	25ml
Cucumber Bitter	1 dash
CBD Syrup	1 pump
Cucumber	1/2

DIRECTIONS

Add all ingredients into glass.

Fill up with ice cubes.

STIR & GARNISH WITH A LONG PEEL OF CUCUMBER.

Best made with ~ Sipsmith Dry Gin

Cool as a Cucumber

DREAM BAGS JAGUAR SHOES

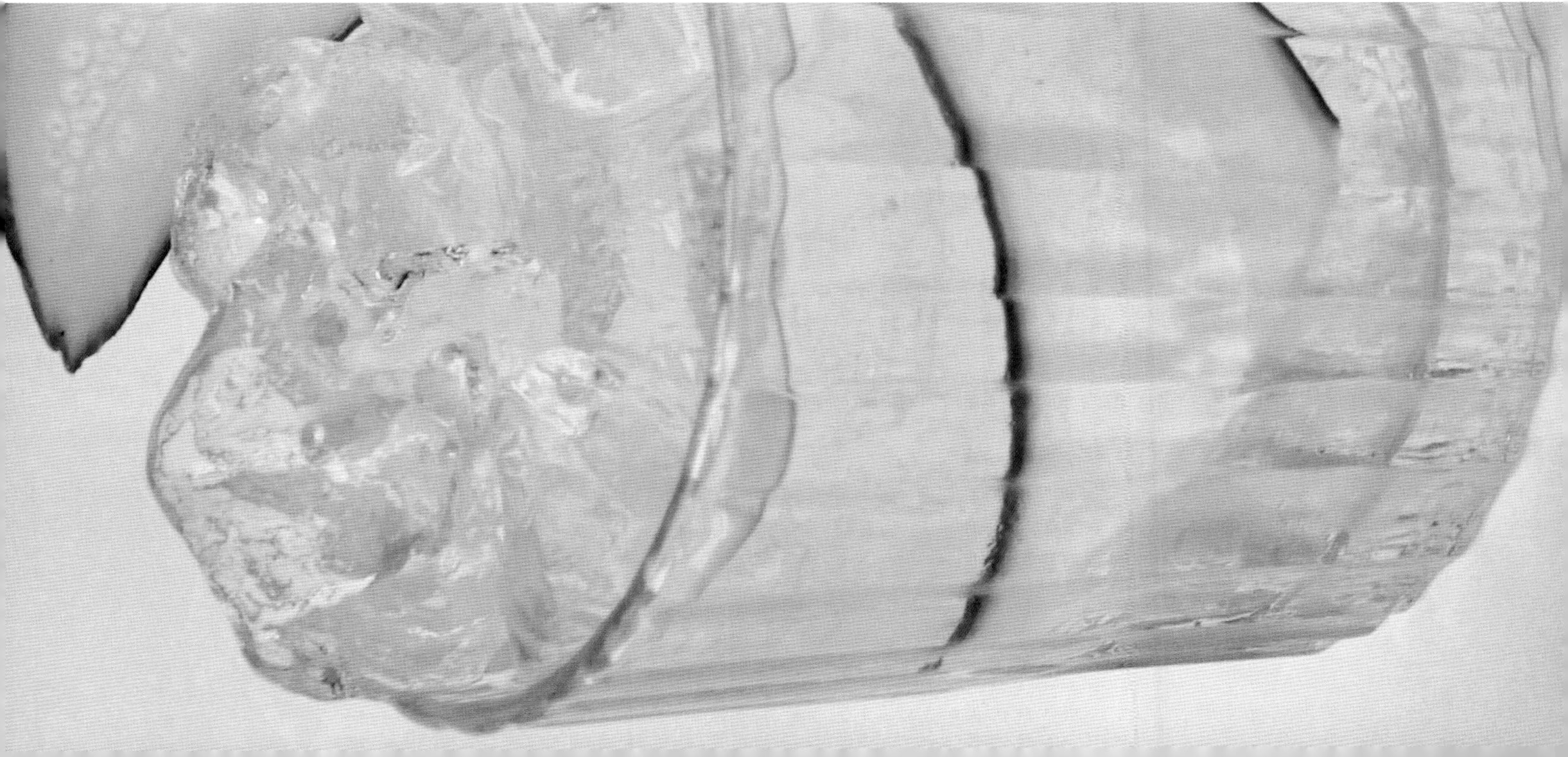

SUNSET SPRITZ

INGREDIENTS

Aperol	10ml
Vermouth	10ml
Esprit De Fig	30ml
Rhubarb Bitter	2 dashes
Prosecco	50ml
Soda	25ml
CBD Syrup	1 pump

GARNISH

Fig	2 slices

TASTE
FRUITY

DIFFICULTY
2/5

GLASS
BALLOON

ELEGANT TAKE ON AN APEROL SPRITZ WITH FIG AND RHUBARB.

The Italian aperitif Aperol was born in Padua in 1919 and created by the Barbieri brothers.

Best made with ~ Noilly Prat Vermouth

DIRECTIONS

Add all ingredients into gin balloon glass.
Fill up with ice cubes and garnish with slices
of fig.

Figgin' Amazing

CHERRY FASHION

This "Old" classic cocktail has a rye, bitters and cherry twist.

MANIFEST GREATNESS

Tastes great with a 5ml dash of Jagermeister Manifest

INGREDIENTS

Whiskey	45ml
Cherry Heering	10ml
Cherry Bitter	2 dashes
CBD Syrup	1 pump
Orange Peel	1
Cherries	2
Large Ice Cubes	1 cup

DIRECTIONS

Add all ingredients to a glass. Stir and add ice, preferably a large circular piece so as not to dilute the cocktail. Give the orange peel a twist to release it's flavour, run it around the edge of the glass and place in the glass. Garnish with two cherries and serve.

Best made with ~ Bulleit Rye Whiskey

AN OLDY BUT A GOODY

In 1880 James E. Pepper, bartender and esteemed bourbon aristocrat, was said to have invented the drink in Louisville, before he brought the recipe to the Waldorf-Astoria Hotel bar in New York City.

For Relaxing Times

TASTE
OAKY

DIFFICULTY
2/5

GLASS
TUMBLER

FLAMINGO DAIQUIRI

Light and dark rum make up this pink tropical and sweet Daiquiri. The name originates from a beach in Cuba and is a word of Taino origin.

The drink was supposedly invented by an American mining engineer named Jennings Cox, during the Spanish–American War of 1898.

A FRESH MOCKTAIL WITH A SOUR TWIST

TASTE
SWEET

DIFFICULTY
3/5

GLASS
COUPETTF

INGREDIENTS

Dark Rum	25ml
Spiced Rum	25ml
Lime Juice	25ml
Pineapple Juice	15ml
Grenadine	20ml
Coconut Water	25ml
CBD Syrup	1 pump

GARNISH

Edible Flower	1

DIRECTIONS

Squeeze out the lime juice.

Shake all ingredients together, apart from the coconut water.

DOUBLE STRAIN INTO A GLASS, TOP WITH COCONUT WATER AND GARNISH WITHA FLOWER.

Best made with ~ Santa Teresa & JAH 45 Rum

INGREDIENTS

White Tequila	40ml
Cointreau	15ml
Grapefruit Juice	30ml
Lime Juice	10ml
Soda	50ml
CBD Syrup	1 pump
Ice Cubes	1 cup

TASTE
SWEET

DIFFICULTY
2/5

GLASS
HIGHBALL

■■☐☐☐

GOLD TEQUILA AND GRAPEFRUIT "LONG" MARGARITA. 100% AGAVE AND SUGAR-FREE TRIPLE SEC GIVES THE COCKTAIL A LOW GI (GLYCEMIC INDEX).

A fizzy cocktail with a bitter-sweet taste and a herbal finish.

GARNISH

| Rosemary | 1 sprig |
| Grapefruit | 1 slice |

Best made with ~ El Jimador Reposado Tequila

DIRECTIONS

Add ingredients, except the soda, to a shaker. Shake and pour into a glass. Top with soda and garnish with dried grapefruit and a fresh sprig of rosemary.

HOW TO MAKE DEHYDRATED FRUIT

It's remarkably easy to dehydrate fruit in the oven. Cut your fruit into 1/2 cm slices and place them in the oven, set to it's lowest possible temperature on a lined tray. Bake for as long as they need, usually 6 - 8 hours.

Easy Peasy

DREAM BAGS JAGUAR SHOES

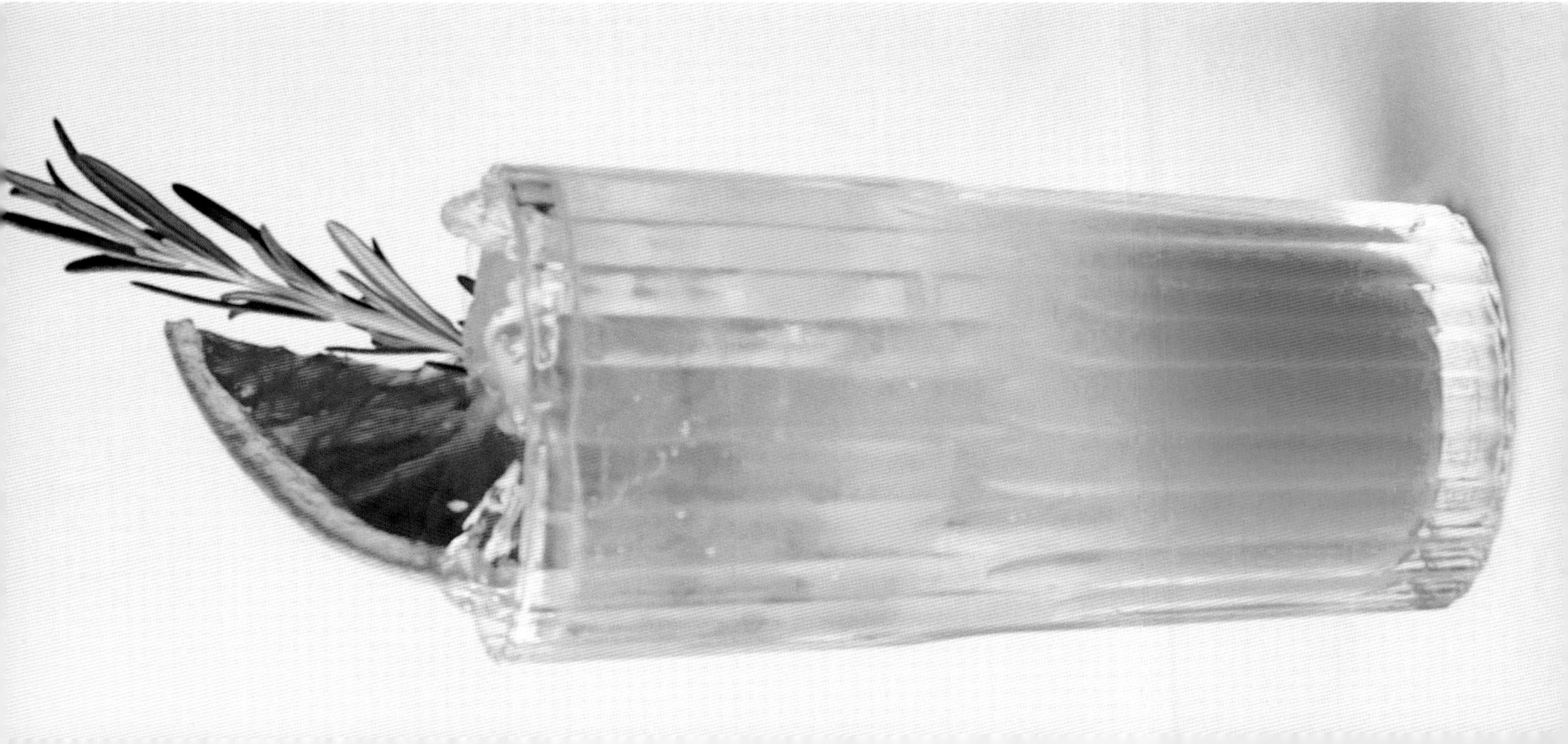

DISCO ESPRESSO

INGREDIENTS

Espresso	50ml
Vodka	25ml
Frangelico	25ml
Chocolate Liqueur	25ml
CBD Syrup	1 pump

TASTE
CHOCOLATE

DIFFICULTY
2/5

GLASS
NICK & NORA

DARK CHOCOLATE AND COFFEE CREATE A RICH AND DECADENT TASTE

GARNISH

Biscuit	1
Chocolate Powder	1 tsp

Best made with ~ Belankaya Vodka & Mozart Dark Liqueur

DIRECTIONS

Shake all ingredients together with ice. Double strain and pour slowly into a chilled glass. Decorate with crumbled biscuit and a dusting of chocolate.

THE ESPRESSO MARTINI

Originally created by Dick Bradsel in a London bar during the 80's. The legend says that a model rumoured to be the young Naomi Cambell asked, "Give me something to wake me up and then f**k me up" and so the Espresso Martini was born.

Wake Me Up

LOCATION SEVEN

DEAR ALICE

THE VIBE

Alice in wonderland meets the great Gatsby in this super secret bar, adorned with stacks of books and 1920's themed decor.

LOCATION

112 ST MARTIN'S LN,
CHARING CROSS,
LONDON
WC2N 4BD

Dear Alice is a mysterious speakeasy, curiously tucked away behind a wardrobe in the basement of LIBRARY Members Club. Once you've found Alice, take a seat and indulge in signature cocktails created by expert in-house mixologists. For those feeling peckish, there are pizzettas and focaccines on the menu with vegan options available.

DEAR ALICE

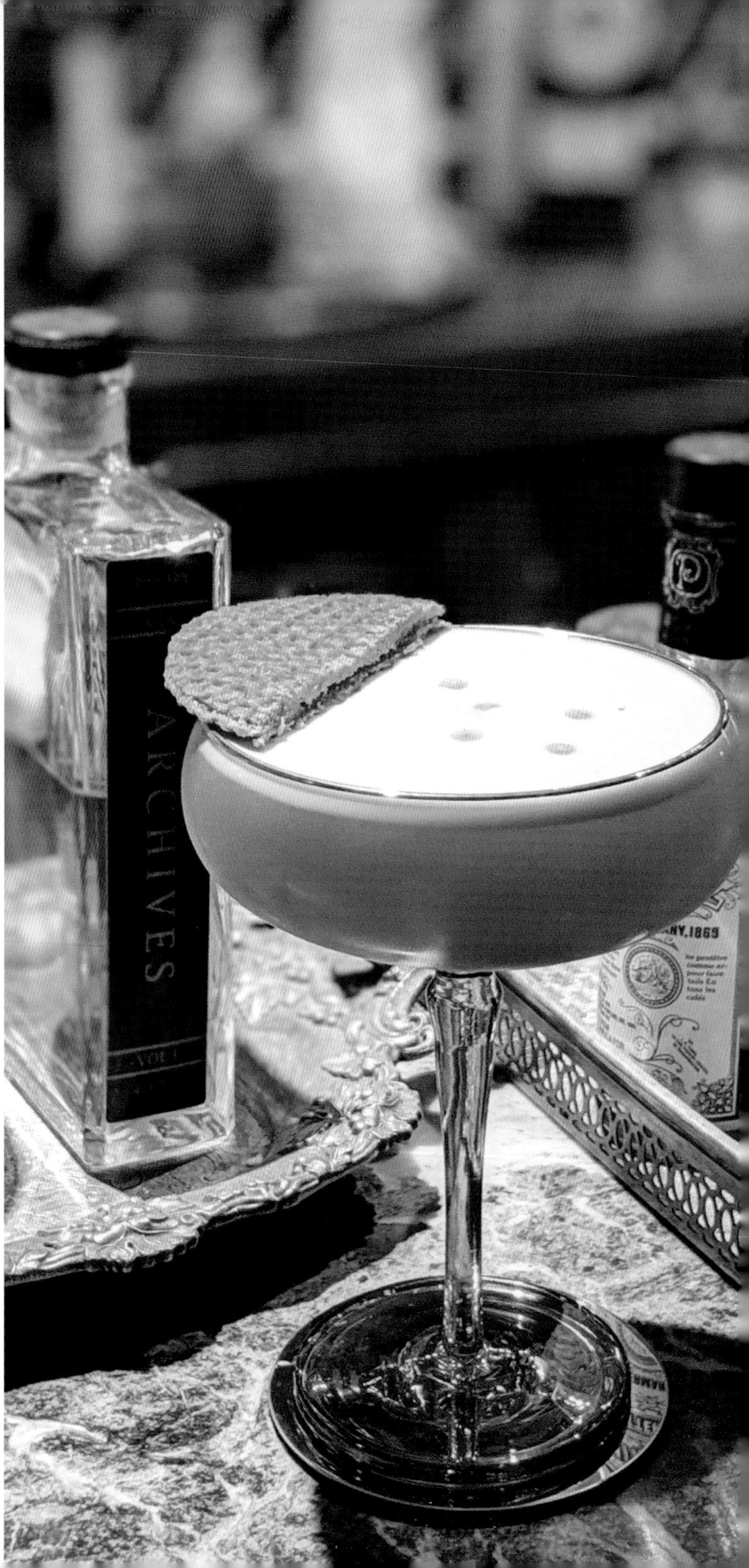

SIX IMPOSSIBLE THINGS
BEFORE BREAKFAST

The Gin Sour is a classic cocktail that predates prohibition in the United States. It has successfully stood the test of time with it's sweet & sour flavour. Our version introduces lavender bitters to complement the taste of CBD.

SIX SWEET & SOUR INGREDIENTS

TASTE
SWEET

DIFFICULTY
3/5

GLASS
COUPETTE

INGREDIENTS

Gin	50ml
Lemon Juice	20ml
Honea	15ml
Aquafaba	20ml
Lavender Bitters	4 dashes
CBD Syrup	2 pump

GARNISH

Caramel Wafer	1

DIRECTIONS

Squeeze out the lemon juice.

Shake ingredients together.

DOUBLE STRAIN INTO GLASS AND GARNISH WITH A CARAMEL WAFER.

Best made with ~ Archives Gin

INGREDIENTS

Bourbon	30ml
Campari	15ml
Pinot Noir	15ml
Vermouth	20ml
Orange Bitter	2 dash
CBD Syrup	1 pump

GARNISH

Orange	1 peel

TASTE
DRY

DIFFICULTY
2/5

GLASS
TUMBLER

WINE AND CITRUS FLAVOUR WITH BITTER NOTES AND A HIGH ALCOHOL VOLUME.

Best made with ~
Bulleit Rye & Carpano Antica Formula

DIRECTIONS

Stir all ingredients together and strain
into a glass filled with ice.
Garnish with an orange peel.

Try infusing your Negroni overnight,
with a few sprigs of thyme.

Drink Me

DEAR ALICE

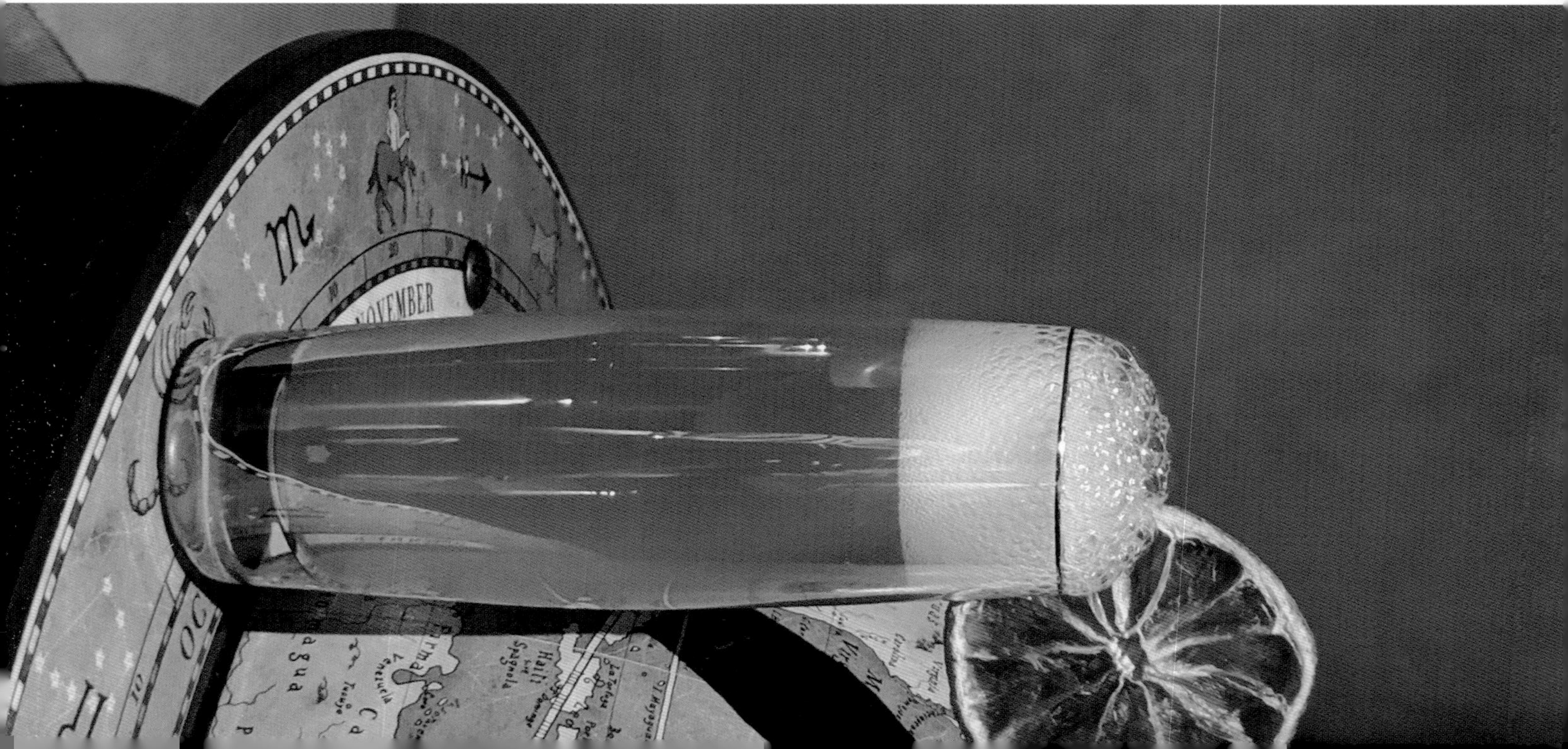

INGREDIENTS

Galliano	15ml
Vodka	30ml
Orange Juice	25ml
Tropical Bitter	2 dash
CBD Syrup	1 pump
Soda	150ml

GARNISH

Orange Wheel	1

TASTE
SWEET

DIFFICULTY
2/5

GLASS
FLUTE

LIGHT, FIZZY AND BUBBLY, WITH A HINT OF ORANGE.

Best made with ~ Ketel One Oranje Vodka

DIRECTIONS

Shake all ingredients together with ice,
double strain and pour slowly into a glass.

Top with soda and garnish
with an orange wheel.

CLARIFIED ORANGE JUICE

For best results try with clarified orange juice, you can make a simple version of this yourself by straining fresh orange juice through muslin cloth. This removes all the nasty bits, leaving a cleaner juice for a clearer cocktail.

Juicy

LOCATION EIGHT

SOANE'S KITCHEN

THE VIBE

An elegant, bright and airy plant-filled space with outdoor seating in a glorious garden.

LOCATION

WALPOLE PARK EALING GREEN,
MATTOCK LN,
EALING,
LONDON
W5 5EQ

Soane's Kitchen is situated in Walpole Park, within Pitzhanger Manor's original walled garden. Come here to escape the City and enjoy fresh and seasonal dishes.

The Dusk of Moscow was created to capture the feeling of watching the sun starting to split the sky, pouring through the buildings, bringing the city to life.

POMEGRANATE POWER

This cocktail is not only refreshing, but has a fiery kick to boot.

INGREDIENTS

Vodka	50ml
Sugar syrup	20ml
Ginger Beer	300ml
CBD Syrup	1 pump
Mint Leaves	8
Pomegranate	1

DIRECTIONS

Firstly, chill down your glass with cubed ice. Once chilled, discard and replenish with fresh cubed ice. Pour in the vodka, then add the pomegranate juice, sugar syrup and CBD. Add in the mint and top the glass with ginger beer. Garnish with mint and pomegranate seeds.

Best made with ~ Ketel One Vodka

POMEGRANATE SYRUP

Why not try making pomegranate syrup to complete the cocktail?
In a medium saucepan, mix 1 litre of pomegranate juice with 100g of sugar and 125ml of lemon juice. Bring to the boil, constantly stirring, until sugar has fully dissolved. Reduce to medium-low heat and simmer until the juice has reduced to 350ml (should take about 1 hour). Leave to cool and decant into an empty bottle.
Store in the fridge for up to 1 month.

TASTE
FIERY

DIFFICULTY
3/5

GLASS
HIGHBALL

S O A N E ' S   K I T C H E N

MELT

THE VIBE

A boutique chocolate-maker, selling creative dark or caramel chocolates, fresh from an open kitchen.

LOCATION

MELT CHOCOLATES
59 LEDBURY RD,
NOTTING HILL,
LONDON
W11 2AA

A fresh chocolate is like nothing else… it truly is sublime. All Melt's recipes are designed in-house. You can watch them making the chocolates in their kitchen inside the store, which is a hub of creative activity. They will only use chocolate that is sourced from companies with strong credentials for supporting the local community and environment. They occasionally run choctail, (chocolate cocktail) making classes, so give them a call if you'd like to take part.

INDULGE

G O   O N ,   Y O U ' V E   E A R N E D   I T

CBD & CHOCOLATE

Infusing chocolate with CBD not only creates a delicious taste, but it allows the CBD to be consumed in an easily digestible form. Whilst the concept of ingesting CBD as a food additive, is still in its infancy, CBD has been used as an natural remedy since time immemorial. By adding CBD to chocolate, we combine the pleasurable sensation of serotonin and theobromine with the added benefits of CBD. Both CBD and chocolate contains cannabinoids, which complements our natural bodies production to create a "taste of earthly paradise".

INGREDIENTS

Kahlúa	30ml
Baileys Almande	30ml
Tequila	30ml
CBD Syrup	1 pump
Dark Chocolate	1 tsp
Chili Flakes	1/2 tsp

TASTE
CHOCOLATE

DIFFICULTY
3/5

GLASS
TUMBLER

When the Spanish conquistadors and the ancient Aztec people collided, the clash of civilizations was on a scale unknown in human history. Ultimately, the wonderful Aztec civilization was destroyed. However, the Flaming Aztec Revenge was their "gift" to the world. This drink is a powerful cocktail containing chocolate, vanilla and chili; all ingredients which arrived with an explosive impact of exotic taste on medieval Europe.

DIRECTIONS

Pour Kahlúa in your glass. Next, begin your layering by slowly and gently pouring each ingredient into your glass. You can do this by pressing the back of a spoon against the side of your glass whilst pouring, to ensure that your layers aren't disrupted. Do this in the following order; Kahlúa, Baileys, tequila and finally topping with a pump of CBD. Garnish by sprinkling with chocolate shavings and chili flakes.

Wars have been fought over Pisco, its origins and the region itself. So we have decided to add passion fruit to the mix, to settle the debate once and for all. This Pisco Passion cocktail captures the spirit of the wonderful Inca civilization, with an exotic passion fruit twist. Smooth, sour and fruity, it exudes an ultimate American, exotic taste.

PISCO HISTORY

The origins of Pisco can be traced back to the days when the Spanish Conquistadors invaded Peru in 1532.

INGREDIENTS

Pisco	50ml
Lime Juice	50ml
Sugar Syrup	50ml
Passion fruit	1
CBD Syrup	1 pump
Aquafaba	50ml
Cubed Ice	1 handful
Angostura Bitters	2 drops
Lime Slice	1

DIRECTIONS

Add the aquafaba to a blender or shaker and shake or blend until the aquafaba starts to stiffen into peaks. Pour the Pisco, lime juice, CBD syrup and sugar syrup into the shaker or blender, along with the beaten aquafaba and ice. Carefully layer the passion fruit in the bottom. Shake vigorously for 30 seconds, or blend for 10, then strain into glass. Add a few drops of Angostura bitters to the top of each cocktail and garnish with a lime slice.

INCA

I N S P I R E D

TASTE
SOUR

DIFFICULTY
3 / 5

GLASS
FLUTE

THE CONDUIT'S SPEAKEASY

THE VIBE

A bar with an exquisitely tiled floor with soft coloured furniture, creates a classy and nostalgic feel of a bygone era.

LOCATION

40 CONDUIT STREET
MAYFAIR
LONDON
W1S 2YQ

Nestled into the cellar level of this building is an intimate venue with a stage for showcasing musicians and other performance artists. Their bar operations manager, Walter Pintus, creates cocktails inspired by the sounds of the Prohibition. The Conduit's Speakeasy is occasionally open to non-members. Reach out to their membership team at membership@theconduit.com for more.

MEMBERS CLUB FOR POSITIVE SOCIAL AND ENVIRONMENTAL CHANGE

A slightly sweeter version of a 'Bamboo Cocktail', with a distinctive nutty profile and an expanding grassy finish. This recipe uses CBD oil, rather than syrup, so that it floats on the surface rather than flavouring the cocktail.

GETTIN' FIGGY WITH IT

Best Made with ~ Beefeater 24 Gin

INGREDIENTS

London Dry Gin	35ml
Mastiha (Fig Infused)	25ml
Absinthe	tsp
Verjus	10ml
CBD Oil	4 drops

DIRECTIONS

Stir all the ingredients over ice in a mixing glass. Strain into a chilled coupette glass. Gently pour 4 separate drops of CBD oil around the surface of the drink, so that they float individually and serve.

FIG LEAF INFUSED MASTIHA

Pour 350ml of Mastiha and 5 large fig leaves in a vacuum bag.
Seal the bag and let it simmer in a saucepan of hot water, over a low temperature of 55 degrees for 3 hours.

Alternatively, infuse for 24 hours at room temperature in a sealed jar.

TASTE
SWEET

DIFFICULTY
4/5

GLASS
COUPETTE

THE CURE

THE VIBE

This hotspot boasts clean lines, beautiful lighting, reclaimed wooden furniture and an enviable plant collection growing from the ceiling.

LOCATION

THE CURE
99 SOUTHGATE RD,
LONDON
N1 3JS

From the team behind The De Beauvoir Deli, The Cure takes its cues from classic LA juice and salad bars. This healthy eatery is all about clean eating and clean living, whilst giving your taste buds something to sing about.

Just Like Heaven is your perfect early morning drink. The citrus cuts through the syrupy goodness of the pineapple to instantly wake you up. In case this is already sounding a bit too much for you, the CBD syrup is there to keep everything smooth and balanced.

READY TO BURST INTO THE DAY

TASTE	DIFFICULTY	GLASS
CITRUS	3/5	LARGE

INGREDIENTS

Pineapple	1/4
Orange	2
Lime	1
Lemon	1/2
Mint	8 leaves
CBD Syrup	1 pump

DIRECTIONS

Cut the pineapple into small chunks and add to a juicer or blender, along with the mint.

Juice the orange, lemon and lime, and add to the pineapple & mint.

ADD ONE PUMP OF LONDON BOTANISTS CBD SYRUP AND MIX THOROUGHLY. POUR OVER ICE, AND SERVE.

JUST LIKE HEAVEN

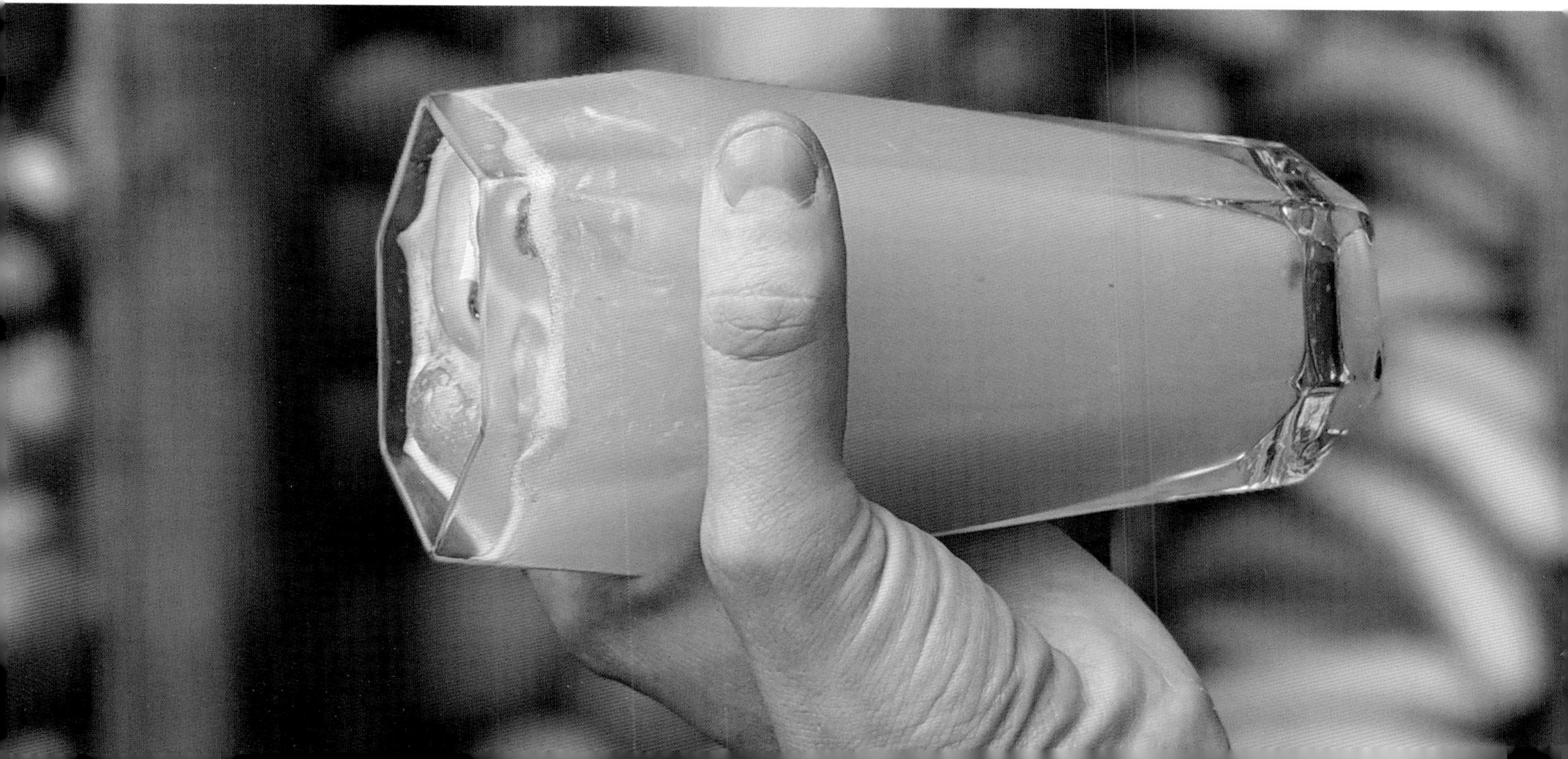

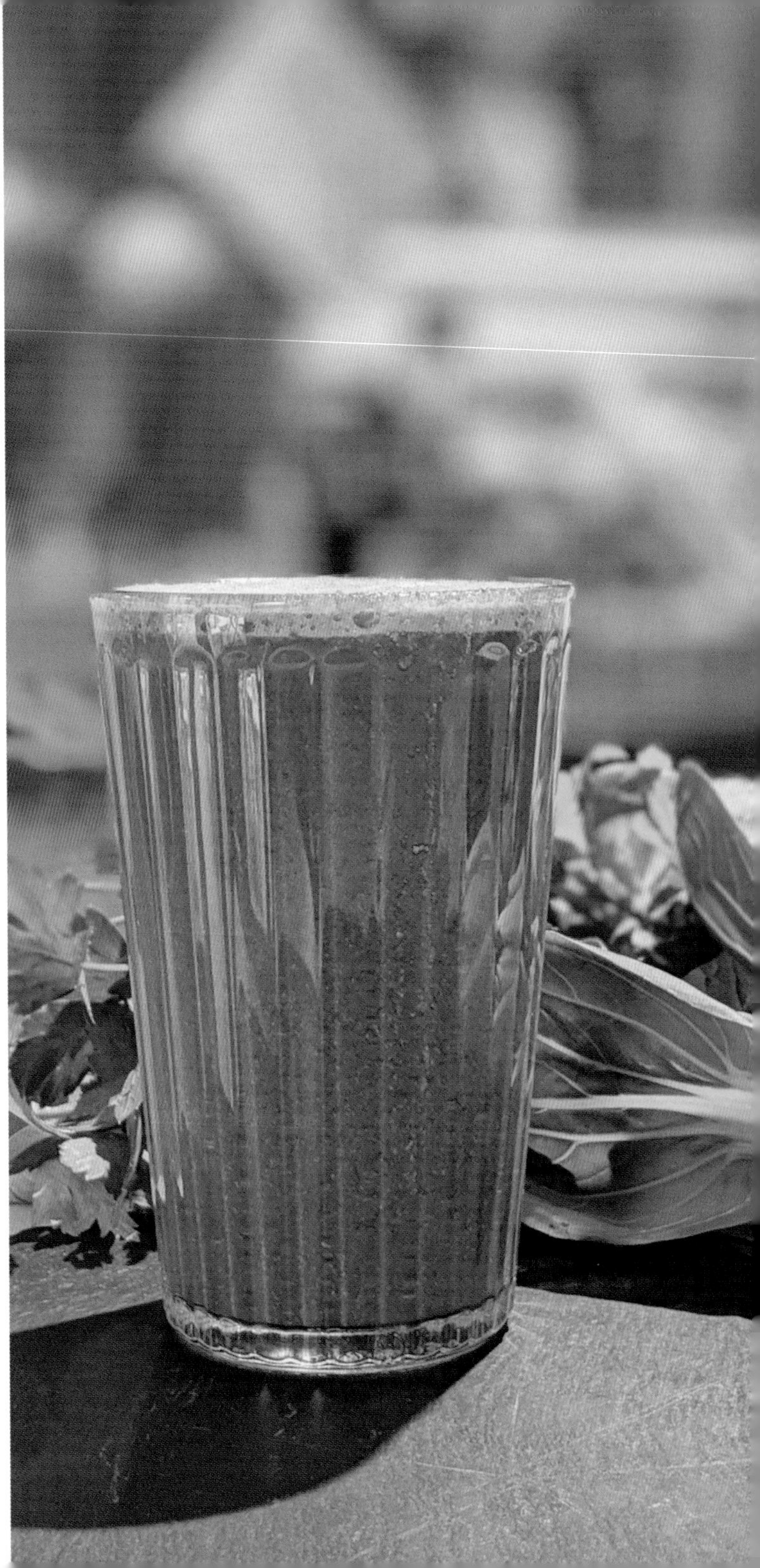

This is the juice that separates the true juicers from the fakers! Imagine the greenest salad ever, juice it, spike it with CBD oil and you have got one hell of a healthy kick coming your way.

GREEN, HEALTHY & FRESH

TASTE
GREEN

DIFFICULTY
2/5

GLASS
LARGE

INGREDIENTS

Kale	100g
Celery	3
Pak Choi	1 head
Spinach	50g
Lemon	1/2
Parsley	15g
Broccoli	1 stalk
CBD Syrup	1 pump

DIRECTIONS

Add all ingredients, minus the lemon to your juicer and blitz.
When including the broccoli, make sure to only use the broccoli stalk and discard the head.

Juice the lemon and add to the blend.

POUR   OVER   ICE

Best made with ~ flat-leaf parsley

BLUSH SMOOTHIE

Blush is the smoothie that wants to care for you, fill you with nutrients, antioxidants, vitamins and general goodness. The pitaya, more commonly known as dragon fruit, is a wonderful way to get some of those essential vitamins and nutrients into your system. Not to mention it is very low in calories, high in dietary fibre and tastes divine.

CLEANSE YOUR SYSTEM

After all these cocktails, it's time to re-balance your system

INGREDIENTS

Pitaya	1/2
Hemp Seeds	1 tsp
Lime	1
Blueberries	1/4 cup
Kale	80g
Spinach	50g
Oat Milk	250ml
CBD Syrup	1 pump

DIRECTIONS

Prepare the Pitaya by slicing in half and scooping out the fruit. Set aside and add all ingredients, (apart from the lime) into your juicer or blender and blend until smooth. Finally, juice the lime and add to the blend.

WHAT ARE ANTIOXIDANTS?

Antioxidants are compounds that inhibit oxidation. Oxidation is a chemical reaction that can produce free radicals, thereby leading to chain reactions that may damage the cells of organisms. Antioxidants such as thiols or ascorbic acid terminate these chain reactions.

Reset

TASTE
ENERGISING

DIFFICULTY
3/5

GLASS
LARGE

BLUSH SMOOTHIE

THANKS & CREDITS

To all the bars which helped make the book possible we'd like to say thankyou! The cocktail recipes you produced are genuinely incredible and the book would not have been possible without your support and hard work.

HICCE
Email: reservations@hicce.co.uk
Phone:**020 3869 8200**

THE BREAKFAST CLUB
Email: henri@themayorofscaredycattown.com
Phone: **020 7078 9639**

THE SPREAD EAGLE
Email: hello@thespreadeaglelondon.co.uk
Phone: **020 8985 0400**

&FEAST
Email: info@andfeast.com
Phone: **020 8748 7000**

BEHIND THIS WALL
Email: alex@behindthiswall.com
Phone: **020 8985 3927**

DREAM BAGS JAGUAR SHOES
Email: dreambags@jaguarshoes.com
Phone: **020 7683 0912**

DEAR ALICE
Email: curious@dear-alice.com
Phone: **020 7240 2874**

SOANE'S KITCHEN
Email: info@soaneskitchen.co.uk
Phone: **020 8579 2685**

MELT
Email: office@meltchocolates.com
Phone: **020 8354 0850**

THE CONDUIT'S SPEAKEASY
Email: membership@theconduit.com
Phone: **020 3912 8400**

THE CURE
Email: info@thecure.shop
Phone: **020 3893 0030**

THE LONDON BOTANISTS
Web: www.thelondonbotanists.com
Email: contact@thelondonbotanists.com
Phone: **020 7129 7568**

ROOT7
Web: www.root7.com
Email: wecare@root7.com
Phone: **020 3923 7481**

IMAGE CREDITS

HICCE - COAL DROPS YARD

INDEX

ROOT7 BARTENDER'S COLLECTION &
THE LONDON BOTANISTS CBD-SYRUP

DESIGNED BY

ROOT7